COOKING
AROUND THE WORLD

An Italian Cookbook for Kids

Rosemary Hankin

PowerKiDS press.

New York

Published in 2014 by The Rosen Publishing Group
29 East 21st Street, New York, NY 10010

Produced for Rosen by Calcium Creative Ltd
Editor for Calcium Creative Ltd: Sarah Eason
US Editor: Sara Howell
Designer: Paul Myerscough

Picture credits: Cover: Shutterstock: GOS Photo Design. Inside: Dreamstime:
Pipa100 7l, Alexander Podshivalov 10, 29t, Yurchyk 7r; Shutterstock: Claudio
Giovanni Colombo 17t, Andras Csontos 25t, Dmitriyorlov 18, 28c, Francesco R.
Iacomino 21b, Inerika 17b, LittleMiss 14, 29c, Maurizio Milanesio 9b, Dmytro
Mykhailov 5tr, Bombaert Patrick 21t, Phant 5tl, Sam Strickler 25b, Viktor1 1, 26,
28b, Nickolay Vinokurov 13t, Vaclav Volrab 9t, Wavebreakmedia 6, Xiong Wei
5b, WhiteRabbit83 22, 29b, Oleg Znamenskiy 13. Tudor Photography: 11, 15,
19, 23, 27.

Library of Congress Cataloging-in-Publication Data

Hankin, Rosemary.
 An Italian cookbook for kids / by Rosemary Hankin
     pages cm. — (Cooking around the world)
 Includes index.
 ISBN 978-1-4777-1336-5 (library binding) — ISBN 978-1-4777-1520-8 (pbk.) —
 ISBN 978-1-4777-1521-5 (6-pack)
 1. Cooking, Italian—Juvenile literature. I. Title.
 TX723.H313 2014
 641.5945—dc23
                                2013003794

Manufactured in the United States of America

CPSIA Compliance Information: Batch #S13PK8: For Further Information contact Rosen Publishing, New York, New York at 1-800-237-9932

Contents

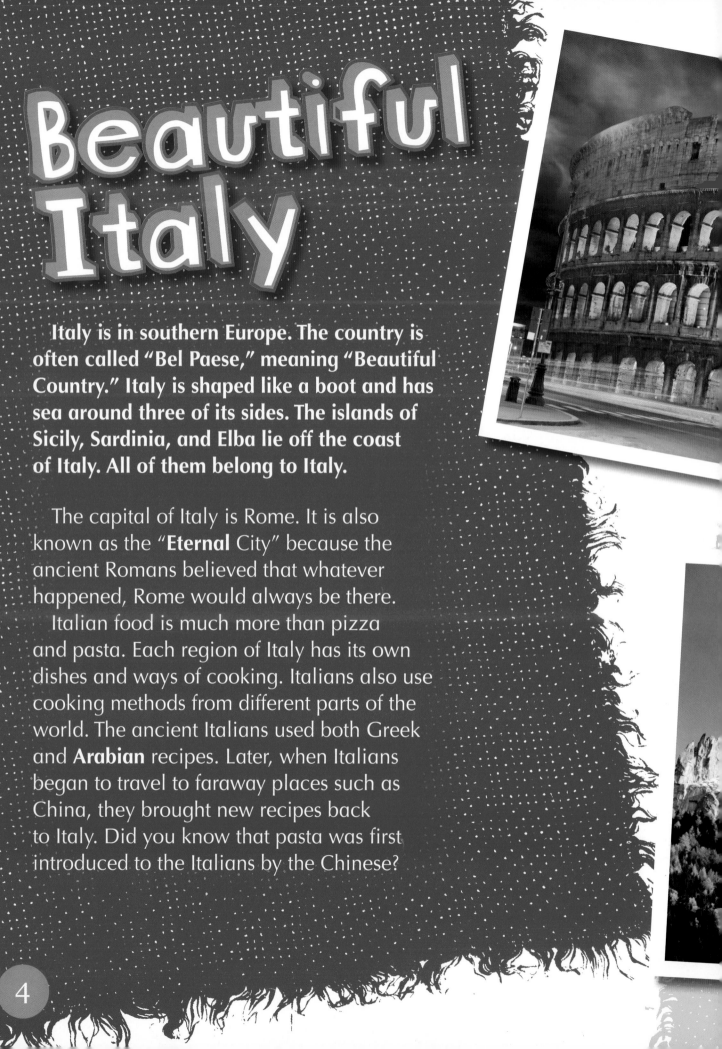

Beautiful Italy

Italy is in southern Europe. The country is often called "Bel Paese," meaning "Beautiful Country." Italy is shaped like a boot and has sea around three of its sides. The islands of Sicily, Sardinia, and Elba lie off the coast of Italy. All of them belong to Italy.

The capital of Italy is Rome. It is also known as the "**Eternal** City" because the ancient Romans believed that whatever happened, Rome would always be there.

Italian food is much more than pizza and pasta. Each region of Italy has its own dishes and ways of cooking. Italians also use cooking methods from different parts of the world. The ancient Italians used both Greek and **Arabian** recipes. Later, when Italians began to travel to faraway places such as China, they brought new recipes back to Italy. Did you know that pasta was first introduced to the Italians by the Chinese?

The Colosseum is in Rome. It was built by the Romans.

Spaghetti Bolognese is one of Italy's most famous dishes. It is spaghetti with a minced beef sauce.

The Dolomites are a mountain range in northeastern Italy.

Get Set to Cook

Cooking is fun! There is nothing better than making food and then sharing it with your family and friends.

Every recipe page in this book starts with a "You Will Need" list. This is a set of **ingredients**. Be sure to collect everything on the list before you start cooking.

Look out for the "Top Tips" boxes. These have great tips to help you cook.

"Be Safe!" boxes warn you when you need to be extra careful.

Use one cutting board for meat and fish and a different cutting board for vegetables and fruit.

Always ask a grown-up if you can do some cooking.

Watch out for sharp knives! Ask a grown-up to help you with chopping and slicing.

Be sure to wash your hands before you start cooking.

Always wash any fruit and vegetables before using them.

Wear an apron to keep your clothes clean as you cook.

Always ask a grown-up for help when cooking on the stove or using the oven.

Mountain Munching

The region of Lombardy is in the north of Italy. The Po River runs through it. There are also lots of famous Italian lakes here, such as the lakes Maggiore, Como, and Garda.

Milanese Style

Milan is the main city in Lombardy. People here eat lots of rice in delicious Milanese risottos, soups, and polenta. They cook with butter and **lard** instead of olive oil. Local people love to eat pork, which is cooked fresh or is made into sausages and salami.

Lombardy is not near the sea, but fish are caught in the streams, rivers, and lakes here. Pike, carp, and **eels** are all used in cooking.

Cheese and Dessert

Many famous cheeses and delicious desserts are made in Lombardy. Creamy mascarpone cheese is used in tiramisu, which means "pick me up." Panettone is a famous Italian Christmas fruitcake that comes from Lombardy. Another dessert is torrone, which is a type of candy made with almonds.

The Italian lakes are a popular vacation resort for both Italians and foreigners.

In Italy, panettone is eaten at Christmas and New Year.

9

Tiramisu

YOU WILL NEED:

3 eggs, separated
3 tbsp superfine sugar
1 pound (453 g)
 mascarpone cheese
1½ cups chocolate milk
24 ladyfingers
chocolate chips or **cocoa**
 powder, to decorate

This delicious, creamy dessert is loved by people all over the world. Grown-ups make tiramisu using strong **espresso** coffee. Here is a recipe for children, which is just as yummy and wickedly chocolaty, too!

BE SAFE!
• The eggs in this dessert are raw so don't serve it to anyone with a health problem.

STEP 1

In a mixing bowl, beat the egg yolks and sugar for around 5 minutes until thick and pale. Add the mascarpone cheese and beat until smooth. Beat in 1 tbsp of the chocolate milk. In a separate bowl, whisk the egg whites until stiff. Gently fold into the mascarpone mixture.

STEP 2

Place the mixture in the base of a 9 x 9 inch (22 x 22 cm) baking dish. Pour the rest of the chocolate milk into a shallow dish. Dip each ladyfinger into the milk.

STEP 3

Place the ladyfingers on top of the marscarpone mixture, standing them upright as shown. Fill the entire dish with the ladyfingers, so that they stand firmly side by side.

STEP 4

Cover with plastic wrap and chill for 2 hours. To serve, sprinkle with chocolate chips or dust with cocoa powder.

TOP TIP Serve this dessert with ripe berries. You could try strawberries, raspberries, or blueberries.

Tuscan Treats

Tuscany is an area with a long coastline on the western side of Italy. It has beautiful beaches and both Italians and foreigners love to come here on vacation. Florence is the main city of the area. It is packed with palaces, churches, museums, and art galleries. There are many amazing places to see, including a bell tower with 414 steps and the Ponte Vecchio, which means "Old Bridge."

Local Cooking

Tuscany is famous for its tasty cheeses, which are made with sheep's milk. One of the best is pecorino. Olive and chestnut trees are grown in Tuscany, and people use lots of olive oil in their cooking. Local people love to eat beans and a spicy ham called prosciutto. Tuscans mainly use vegetables such as artichokes, asparagus, and **fennel** in their cooking. Many recipes use duck, rabbit, and **wild boar**, flavored with rosemary, sage, and thyme.

Dip, Break, Eat!

Bread is eaten in many different ways. On its own, it is dipped in rich olive oil. Bread is also put into soups and used in salads. *Panzanella* is a salad made with broken-up bread, onions, tomatoes, and basil.

Florence is a beautiful city that is full of wonderful old buildings.

Tuscany has many olive groves. The olives are eaten and **pressed** into delicious olive oil.

13

Minestrone Soup

YOU WILL NEED:

8 tbsp olive oil

1 small onion, chopped

7½ cups ham stock

3½ pounds (1½ kg) vegetables, such as beets, carrots, cauliflower, celery, garlic, leeks, parsnips, and potatoes, chopped

1 x 15 ounce (425 g) can borlotti beans, drained and rinsed

2 tomatoes, skinned and chopped

1 cup pasta shapes

salt and ground black pepper, to taste

Minestra means "soup" in Italian. This soup is made all over Italy, and each region has its own recipe. You can use any number of vegetables and different pasta shapes. Serve with crusty bread.

BE SAFE!
- Be careful when opening the can of beans.
- Ask a grown-up to help you to prepare the vegetables.

14

STEP 1

Heat the oil in a large pan. Fry the onion until soft, then add the stock and bring to a boil. Meanwhile, wash and peel the vegetables, as necessary, then chop into evenly sized pieces.

STEP 2

Add the vegetables to the pan (see Top Tip) and bring to a simmer. Cook for 20 minutes, then add the tomatoes. Cook for 30 minutes more, then check to make sure that all the vegetables are cooked.

STEP 3

Around 20 minutes before the dish is finished, add the pasta shapes and beans. Bring back to a simmer, and cook until the vegetables are cooked but are still firm.

STEP 4

Add salt and pepper to taste, then serve hot with lots of crusty bread for dipping.

TOP TIP Add carrots, potatoes, parsnips, and beets to the pan first. They take longest to cook.

Middle Italy

The region of Lazio is right at the center of Italy. It stretches from the mountains to the sea. Lazio has an amazing history and the capital city of Rome is here. Many people think Rome was first built as far back as 750 BC! The Romans visited many places around the world and brought back the recipes they discovered abroad. Many of the dishes made in Lazio are a mix of cooking ideas and styles from different countries around the world.

Farming and Fishing

Lazio has plenty of good farmland. Cows, pigs, sheep, and chickens are all raised here. Potatoes, artichokes, zucchini, garlic, tomatoes, and olives are grown in Lazio. On the coast, fishermen catch fresh **anchovies**. Mozzarella cheese is the area's most famous cheese. This cheese has a rubbery texture and is traditionally made with water buffalo milk.

Celebrating Food

Italians love their food, and they love to celebrate, too. In June each year there is a cherry **festival** in the village of Celleno. The local people make cakes, candy, and pies using cherries. They also put on parades with lots of music and dancing.

Lazio has lots of green pastures in which farmers keep their sheep and cows.

Mozzarella is usually made with water buffalo milk. Today, it is sometimes also made using cow's milk.

17

Crunchy Chicken

YOU WILL NEED:

4 tbsp olive oil

1 cup buttermilk

1½ pounds (680 g) skinless, boneless chicken breast fillets, sliced into 18 pieces

1¼ cups Parmesan, freshly grated

¾ cup **seasoned** bread crumbs

fresh parsley sprigs, to **garnish**

These pieces of chicken have a lovely, crunchy coating that is mixed with tasty Parmesan cheese. Garnish with parsley and serve with a crisp mixed salad, tossed in a homemade Italian salad dressing.

BE SAFE!
• Ask a grown-up to help you chop the chicken.

STEP 1

Preheat the oven to 475°F (240°C). Line two baking sheets with parchment paper, then brush 1 tbsp of the olive oil over each.

STEP 2

Place the buttermilk in a bowl. Add the chicken pieces and stir to coat them. Let them stand for 30 minutes. Meanwhile, stir together the Parmesan and seasoned bread crumbs in a mixing bowl.

STEP 3

Remove the chicken pieces from the buttermilk and roll them in the bread crumb mixture. Make sure they are coated. Arrange the coated chicken pieces on the prepared baking sheets, spacing them well apart. **Drizzle** the remaining 2 tbsp olive oil over the chicken pieces.

STEP 4

Bake in the preheated oven for around 12 minutes, until cooked through. Transfer to a serving plate and garnish with sprigs of fresh parsley.

TOP TIP If you cannot find buttermilk, mix equal parts of low-fat milk and plain yogurt.

Land of Pizza

Naples is the main city of an area called Campania. One of the world's most famous **volcanoes**, Vesuvius, is nearby. The area around it has lots of great farming land because the soil is so rich. The coastline here is called the Amalfi Coast and fishermen catch wonderful fresh fish and seafood along it.

Pizza and Pasta Heaven

The city of Naples is famous all over the world for being the home of the pizza. Cooks put tomatoes, basil, and mozzarella onto a bread base to make a classic pizza. Campania also has lots of different kinds of pasta. Tube pastas, macaroni, and spaghetti are eaten with tasty local tomato sauces.

Sweet Treats

Local people love their ice cream, which is called gelato. Honey-coated *struffoli* puffs are also popular. Zeppole is a special doughnut that is made with ricotta cheese and served on St. Joseph's Day in March.

Simple pizzas often taste the best. This one is topped with cheese, tomatoes, onions, and fresh basil.

Fishermen catch fish and seafood along the beautiful Amalfi Coast.

Margherita Pizza

YOU WILL NEED:

2½ cups strong bread flour
1 tsp instant yeast
1 tsp salt
1 cup warm water
1 tbsp olive oil, plus extra
   for drizzling
½ cup plain tomato sauce
1 garlic clove, minced
salt and ground black
   pepper, to taste
4 ounces (113 g) mozzarella,
   sliced
4 ounces (113 g) Parmesan,
   grated
fresh basil leaves,
   to garnish

You can have simple toppings on a pizza, or you can add lots of different foods. The Margherita pizza is an easy way to get started with pizza making. It simply uses tomato, basil, and cheese.

BE SAFE!
- Ask a grown-up to help you use the oven.
- Always use oven mitts.

STEP 1

Flour two baking sheets. For the base, sift the flour, yeast, and salt into a mixing bowl. Make a well in the center. Pour in the water and oil. Stir to form a soft dough. Turn onto a floured surface and knead for 5 minutes. Cover and set aside in a warm place for an hour to make the dough rise.

STEP 2

Preheat the oven to 450°F (230°C). Mix the tomato sauce and garlic, then season with salt and ground black pepper. Set the mixture aside.

STEP 3

Divide the dough into two pieces. On a floured work surface, roll each piece out to a 10 inch (25 cm) round. Place on the baking sheets.

STEP 4

Spoon the tomato sauce over the bases. Add the mozzarella and Parmesan. Season and drizzle with olive oil. Bake each pizza in the preheated oven on the top shelf for 8–10 minutes. Garnish with basil.

TOP TIP You can also buy the pizza bases and just add your favorite toppings!

Sicilian Feasts

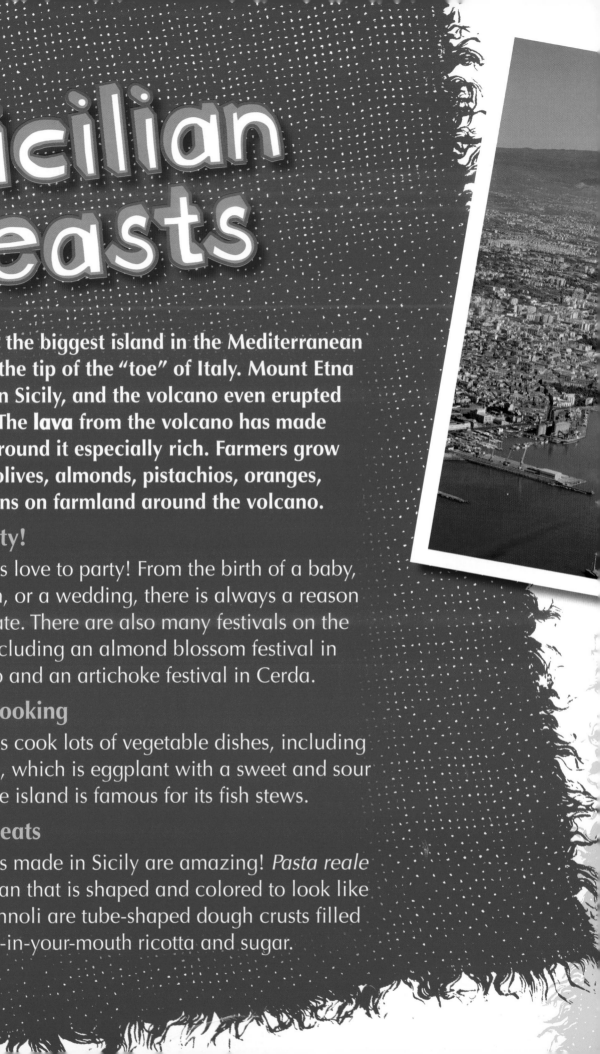

Sicily is the biggest island in the Mediterranean and is at the tip of the "toe" of Italy. Mount Etna is found in Sicily, and the volcano even erupted recently. The **lava** from the volcano has made the soil around it especially rich. Farmers grow crops of olives, almonds, pistachios, oranges, and lemons on farmland around the volcano.

Let's Party!

Sicilians love to party! From the birth of a baby, a baptism, or a wedding, there is always a reason to celebrate. There are also many festivals on the island, including an almond blossom festival in Agrigento and an artichoke festival in Cerda.

Island Cooking

Sicilians cook lots of vegetable dishes, including caponata, which is eggplant with a sweet and sour sauce. The island is famous for its fish stews.

Sweet Treats

Desserts made in Sicily are amazing! *Pasta reale* is marzipan that is shaped and colored to look like fruits. Cannoli are tube-shaped dough crusts filled with melt-in-your-mouth ricotta and sugar.

Smoke from Mount Etna can be seen in the background in this picture of Sicily.

Cannoli al Cioccolato
farina "00" - margarina - acqua - sale
lievito - zucchero - olio vegetale - nocciole
latte - cacao.
€1.50 cad

Wonderful desserts, such as these *cannoli al cioccolato*, are eaten in Sicily.

Fusilli

YOU WILL NEED:

4 cups fusilli

1 x 6 ounce (170 g) can tuna chunks in oil

ground black pepper, to taste

4 ounces (113 g) cherry tomatoes, whole or cut in half

5 ounces (141 g) Taleggio or Fontina cheese, finely chopped

fresh basil leaves, to garnish

Fusilli is pasta that has been formed into short spiral shapes. It is often sold in **tricolor** packets containing yellow, orange, and green pieces. Here it is baked with tuna and tomatoes, then topped with Italian cheese.

BE SAFE!
• Ask a grown-up to help you with this recipe.
• Let the dish cool for a few minutes before serving.

STEP 1

Cook the pasta in plenty of boiling salted water, following the packet instructions. Drain and place in an ovenproof dish. Then toss with a little of the tuna oil to moisten well, and set aside. Preheat the oven to 400°F (200°C).

STEP 2

In a bowl, flake the tuna using a fork, then gently stir it into the pasta. Season with ground black pepper, if using. Tuck the whole or halved cherry tomatoes into the dish. Scatter the cheese evenly over the top.

STEP 3

Cover the dish loosely with foil. Place in the center of the oven and bake for 20 minutes. Take off the foil and bake for 10–15 minutes more, or until piping hot and beginning to brown on the top.

STEP 4

Let the dish cool for 10 minutes before serving, garnished with fresh basil.

TOP TIP Choose a harder cheese if you wish, such as Monterey Jack, and grate it over the pasta.

27

Italian Meals on the Map!

Switzerland

River Po

France

Crunchy Chicken

Now that you have discovered how to cook the delicious foods of Italy, find out where they are cooked and eaten on this map of the country.

Fusilli

Lombardy

Tiramisu

Tuscany

Minestrone
Soup

Lazio

ROME

Naples

Italy

Margherita Pizza

Mediterranean
Sea

Sicily

Glossary

anchovies (AN-choh-veez) Very salty fish that are used to add flavor to salads, pizzas, and other dishes.

Arabian (uh-RAY-bee-un) From Arabic areas such as Iran and Iraq.

cocoa (KOH-koh) A powder that is made from cocoa pods and used to flavor food.

drizzle (DRIH-zul) To lightly pour a liquid such as oil over food.

eels (EELZ) Very long fish that look a little like snakes.

espresso (eh-SPREH-soh) A very strong coffee.

eternal (ih-TUR-nul) To live forever.

fennel (FEH-nul) A bulb-shaped, tangy-tasting vegetable.

festival (FES-tih-vul) A large celebration in which many people take part.

garnish (GAR-nish) To decorate food before serving.

ingredients (in-GREE-dee-untz) Different foods and seasonings that are used to make a recipe.

lard (LARD) A hard, white fat that is used in cooking in place of butter, margarine, or oil.

lava (LAH-vuh) Very hot liquid rock that pours from volcanoes.

pressed (PRESD) Squeezed hard until the juices run out.

seasoned (SEE-zund) Food that has salt and pepper added to it.

tricolor (TRY-kul-er) Made up of three colors.

volcanoes (vol-KAY-nohz) Openings in the Earth's crust from which lava flows.

wild boar (WYLD BOR) A wild pig that lives mainly in forests.

Further Reading

Gioffre, Rosalba. *Fun with Italian Cooking*. Let's Get Cooking!
   New York: PowerKids Press, 2010.

Goodman, Polly. *Food in Italy*. Food Around the World.
   New York: PowerKids Press, 2008.

Wagner, Lisa. *Cool Italian Cooking: Fun and Tasty Recipes for Kids*. Cool World Cooking. Minneapolis, MN:
   Checkerboard Books, 2011.

Websites

Due to the changing nature of Internet links, PowerKids Press has developed an online list of websites related to the subject of this book. This site is updated regularly. Please use this link to access the list:
www.powerkidslinks.com/caw/ital

Index